PUPPY

GLASSES GANG

COLORING BOOK FOR ADULTS

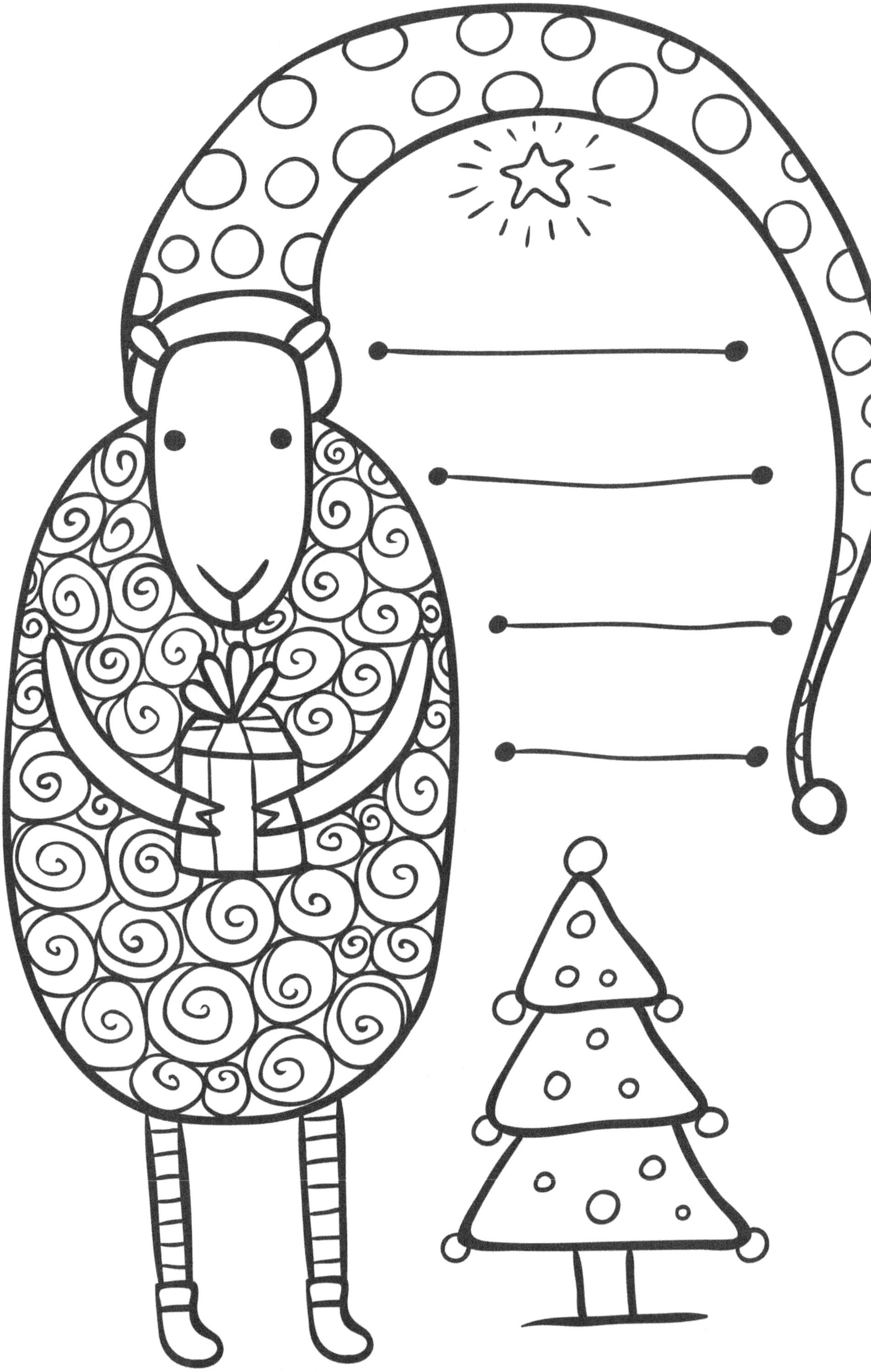

HIPSTER STYLE

HIPSTER
STYLE

We're all mad here

MORE
Hipster
Style

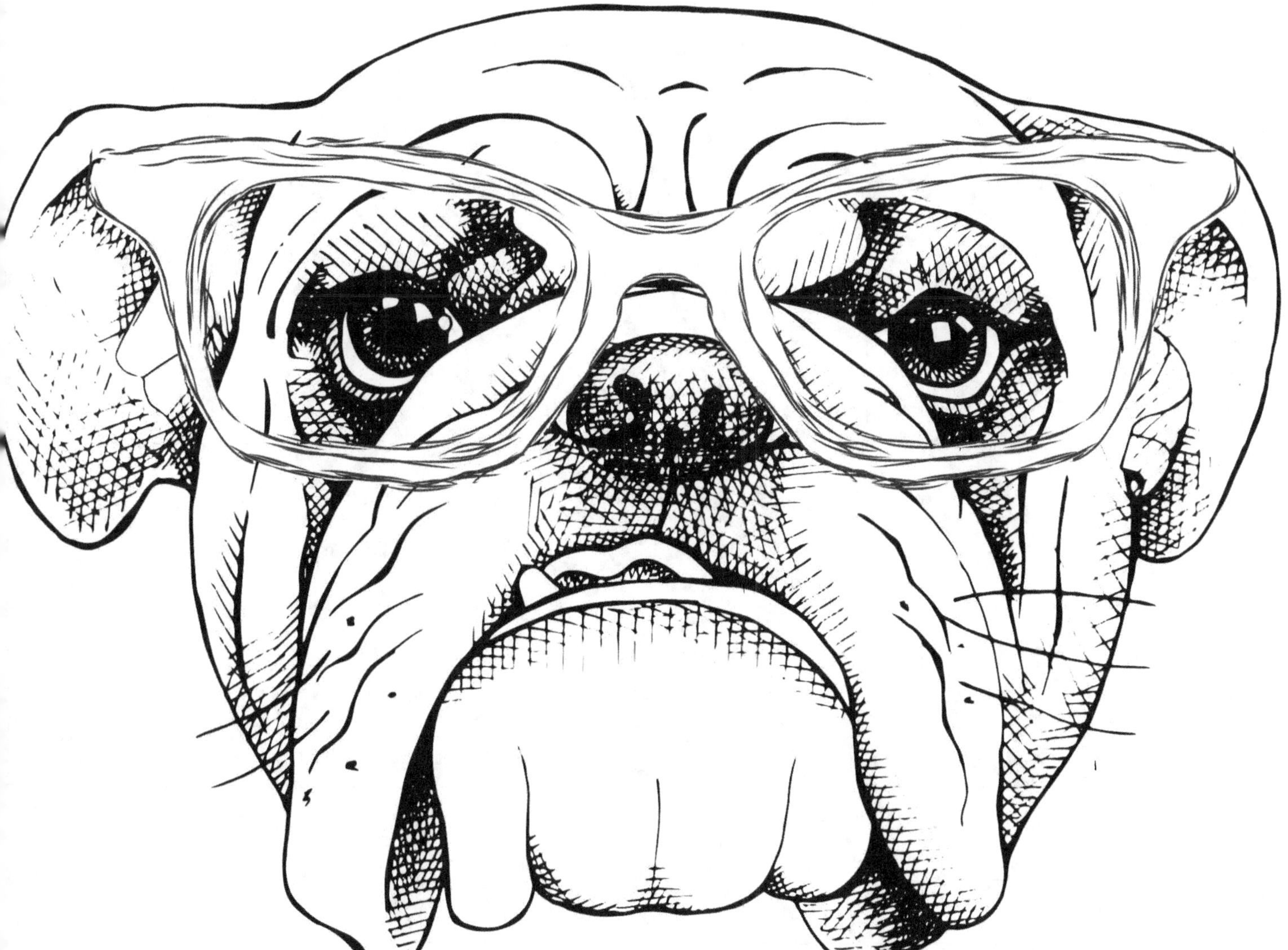

I will love you forever!

woof
READY to SKI!

Monkey
Business

Sun Beach

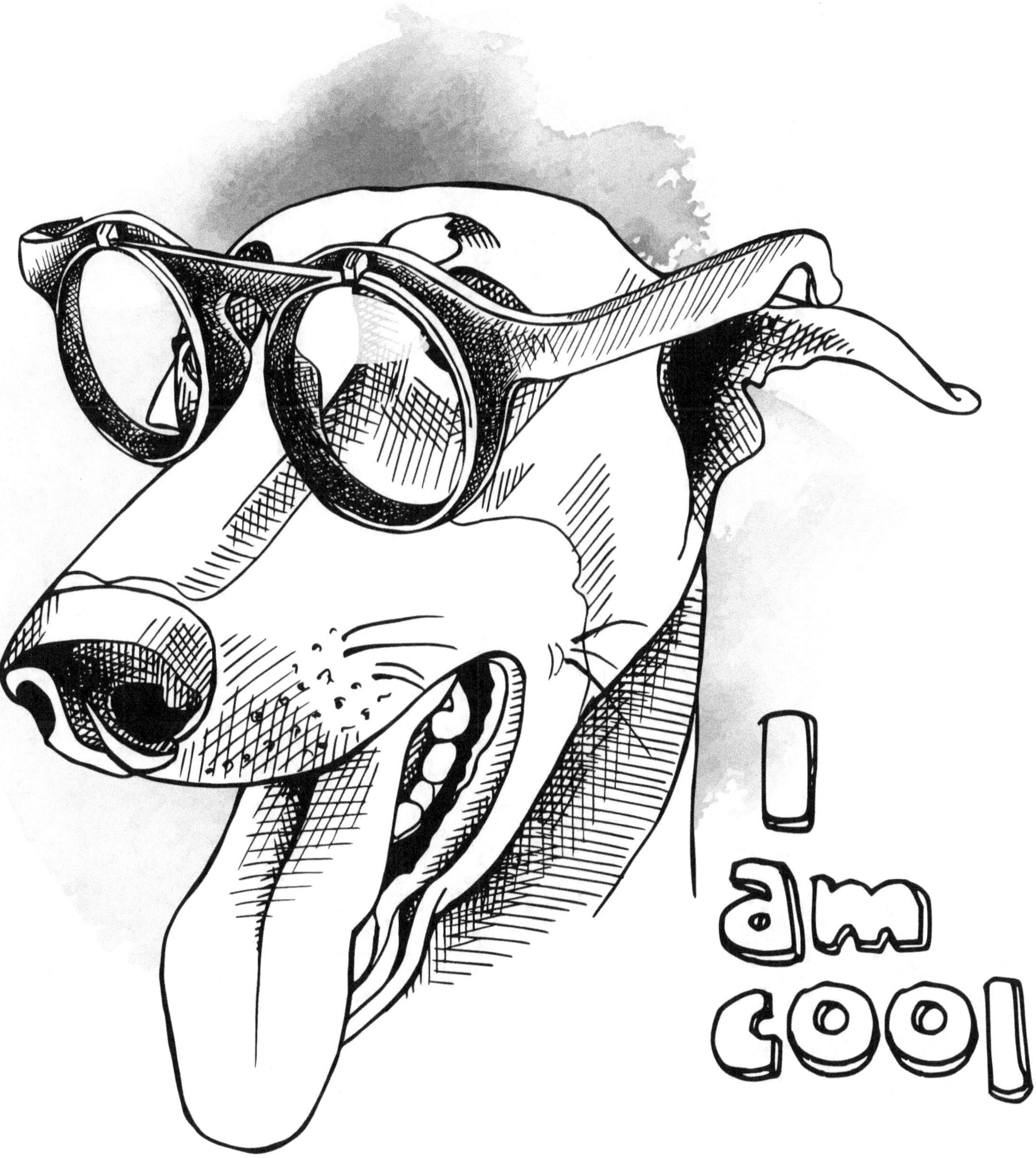
I am cool

READY to SKI!

MERRY
CHRISTMAS

NY
CITY

HIPSTER
STYLE

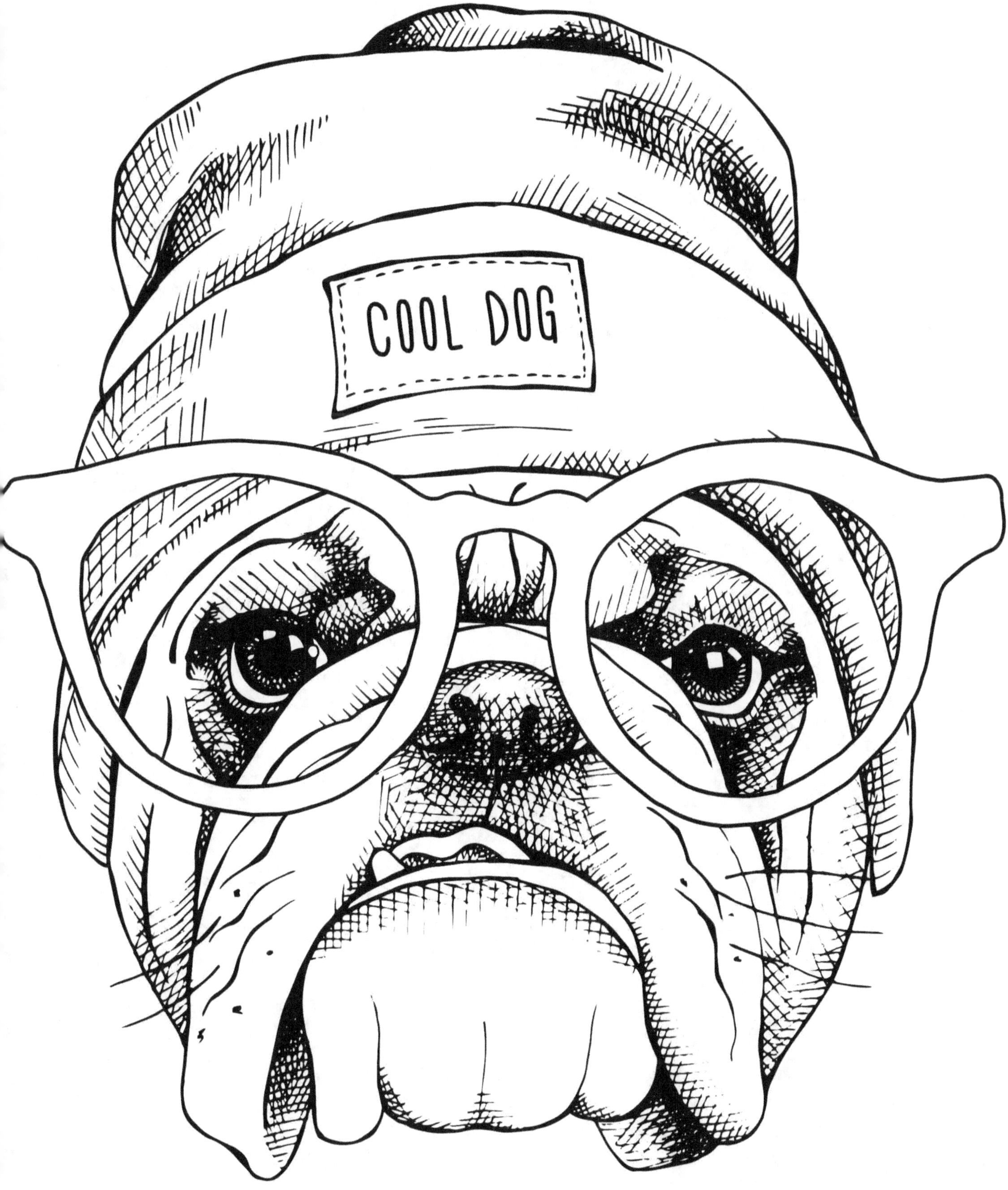
COOL DOG

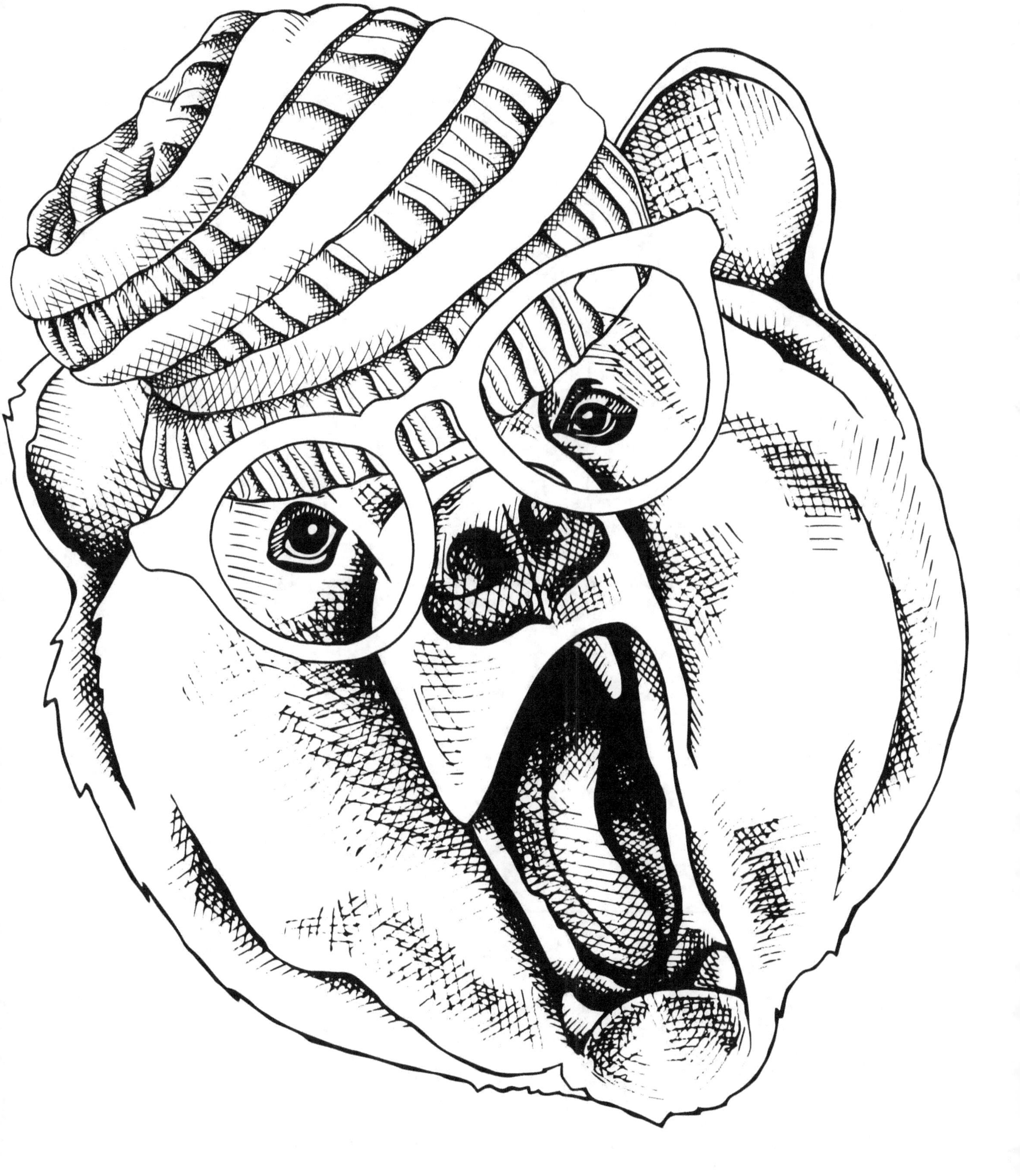

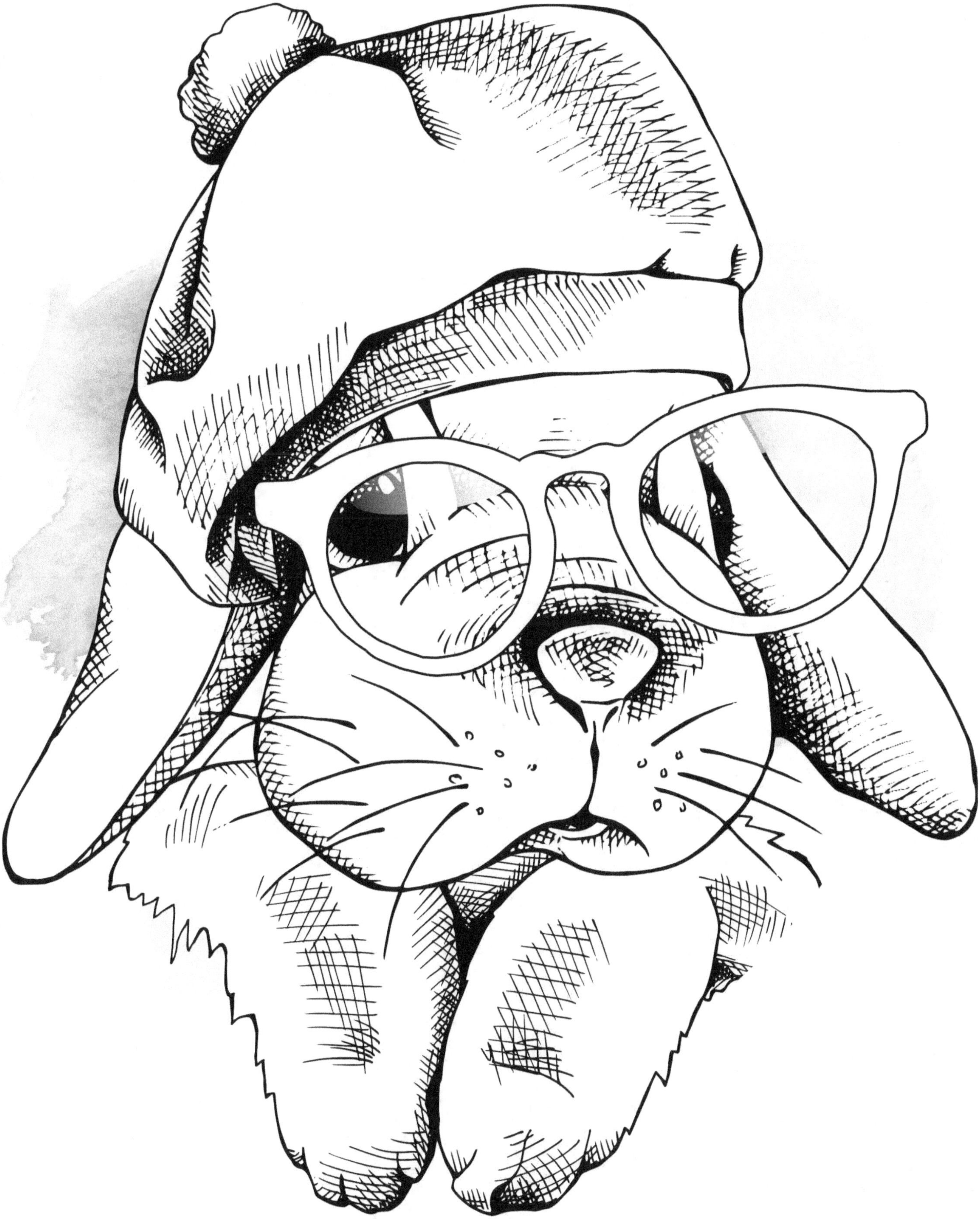

Ho, ho, ho Y'all!

I ♥ giraffe

COOL

free download

At : bit.ly/get_sample_free

V Art Studio

www.ingramcontent.com/pod-product-compliance
Lightning Source LLC
Chambersburg PA
CBHW080834310526
45788CB00020B/3525
* 9 7 8 1 5 4 6 8 3 1 3 1 0 *